Tell me about...

Basketball

Belmont
THE RIDGEWAY, MILL HILL

LEARNING RESOURCES CENTRE
Telephone: 020 8906 7270

Published in 2009 by Evans Publishing Ltd,
 2A Portman Mansions,
Chiltern St, London WIU 6NR

© Evans Brothers Limited 2009

Editor: Nicola Edwards
Designer: D.R. Ink
All photographs by Wishlist except for page 6 Glenn James/NBAE via Getty Images; page 8 Jesse D.
Garrabrant/NBAE via Getty Images; page 10 Bryan Bedder/Getty Images; page 12 Jesse D.
Garrabrant/NBAE/Getty Images; page 13 Andrew D. Bernstein /NBAE via Getty Images; page 16
Timothy A. Clary/AFP/Getty Images; page 21 Bill Baptist/NBAE via Getty Images; page 23 Streeter
Lecka/Getty Images; page 23 Copyright 2008 NBAE (Photo by Garrett Ellwood/NBAE via Getty Images);
page 26 Copyright 1998 NBAE (Photo by Andrew D. Bernstein/NBAE via Getty Images; page 27
Copyright 2008 NBAE (Photo by Andrew D. Bernstein/NBAE via Getty Images

British Library Cataloguing in Publication Data

 Gifford, Clive
   Basketball. - (Tell me about sport)
   1. Basketball - Juvenile literature
   I. Title
   796.3'23

ISBN-13: 9780237537258

Printed in China.

Printed on chlorine free paper from sustainable sources.

Contents

Basketball

Top basketball players are spectacular athletes. They can leap high and react quickly to perform amazing moves.

Basketball is a high-scoring, action-packed team sport. Players pass, catch and dribble a basketball (by bouncing it as they run) around a court. Each team scores points by shooting the ball through a basket which stands 3.05 metres above the ground.

A basketball team has as many as twelve players but only five are allowed on the court at one time. A team's coach can switch players on and off the court throughout the game.

Different basketball competitions have different rules, but most games for adults last 40 or 48 minutes and are divided into two halves or four quarters. This may not sound long, but play moves very quickly and most players are exhausted when the final buzzer ends the game.

Basketball is exciting to watch. The action is fast and intense. Millions watch top players in North America's NBA (National Basketball Association) league and at the Olympic Games.

Basketball is also great fun to play. Most of the top players are very tall, standing over two metres. But you don't have to be a giant to play and enjoy the sport. Young players starting out can play a smaller version of the game called mini basketball.

▲ You will often be asked to come off the court to be substituted by a team-mate. Don't be upset. There's every chance you will be back on the court a few minutes later.

▼ The team in the white shirts is on the attack. One player bounces and controls the ball whilst his team-mates move into space to receive a pass.

Scoring a basket

▲ Playing for the United States team at the 2008 Olympics, LeBron James is about to score a basket. The ball must travel down through the hoop for a basket to count. The board behind the hoop and the net is called the backboard.

Nothing beats the feeling of seeing your shot sail through the hoop to score a basket. Every player on a team needs to be able to shoot well. This means that shooting will be a large part of your basketball training.

Players learn to score with different shots. In the set shot, players stand still with their hand behind and slightly underneath the ball. They stretch their arm up and release the ball with a flick of their wrist. Other shots, such as lay ups (see page 19), are made on the move.

A successful shot can be worth one, two or three points. To score a 'three pointer', you have to take your shot from beyond a line on the court called the three point line (see page 10).

A shot from closer in during regular play wins two points and a free throw is worth one point. One or more free throws are awarded when the other team has broken the rules.

▶

A jump shot is a common shot in basketball. You jump straight up and release the ball at the top of the jump.

▼

You are just under five metres away from the basket when you take a free throw. Other players from both teams stand around the edge of the key (see pages 10-11).

Scoring superstars

The American basketball star Kareem Abdul-Jabbar scored 38,387 points in his NBA career, the highest total of any player.

In 1962, Wilt Chamberlain scored an incredible 100 points in a single NBA match!

The court and kit

Basketball can be played on an inside court in a gym or on an outside court in a park or school playground. The lines round the edge of the court are out of play. This means that if the ball bounces on them, then the ball has left the court.

A full size court is cut into two by a halfway line. The half containing the basket that your team wants to attack is your front court. The other half is your back court.

If your team gets the ball in your back court, you have 8 or 10 seconds (depending on which rules you are using) to cross the halfway line. If you don't manage this, the ball is

▼ A basketball court is 28.5m long in the NBA and 28m long in many other competitions. The shaded area is called the key.

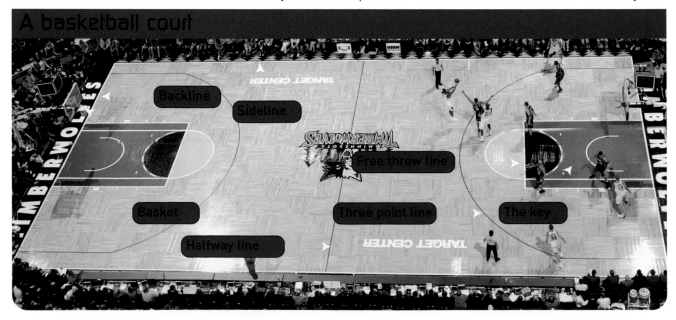

A basketball court

Backline

Sideline

TARGET CENTER

Free throw line

Basket

Three point line

The key

Halfway line

TARGET CENTER

passed to the other team. Once you move over the halfway line with the ball, you cannot return to the back court.

The basket, made up of a hoop and net, overhangs the court. Below it is a marked out area called the key. Attacking players aren't allowed to stand in this area for more than three seconds at a time.

One of the many great things about basketball is that you don't need lots of equipment to play – just shorts, a vest and well-fitting trainers.

Court and ball

The first baskets were real baskets used for carrying peaches. They were nailed to the wall by the sport's inventor, James Naismith, an American P.E. teacher, in 1891.

In 1979, Darryl Dawkins slammed the ball so hard through the basket that the glass backboard shattered! He did this twice in three weeks, earning the nickname 'the Master Blaster'.

▼

A basketball game starts with one player from each side competing at a jump ball. The ball is thrown into the air and both players try to tap it to one of their team-mates.

▼

When the ball leaves the court and the other team touched it last, your team gets the ball. You put it back into play by throwing it in from the sideline.

Star players

The world's top players are professional which means they are paid to play basketball. In the USA especially they are massive celebrities, just like film and music stars. Behind the glitz and the glamour, though, there is plenty of hard work.

▼ Los Angeles Lakers players, Kobe Bryant (number 24) and Vladimir Radmanovic (number 10) compete with the Boston Celtics' Paul Pierce in the 2008 NBA Finals. The Celtics won the Finals by four games to two.

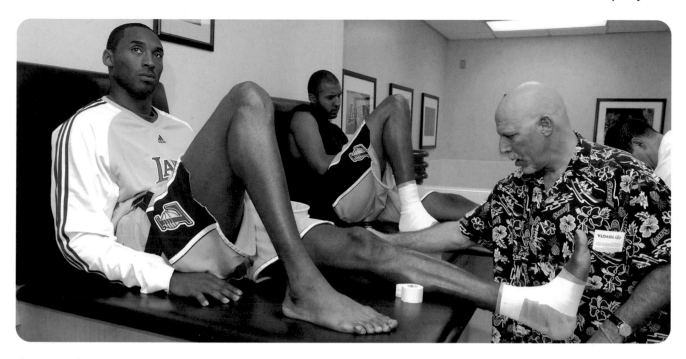

▲ Injuries can be damaging to a star player's career. NBA superstar, Kobe Bryant, sits on the treatment table as his team's trainer checks his leg. His ankle is taped to give it extra support.

NBA stars train hard and need to be incredibly fit. This is because they have a long and punishing season ahead. The regular season begins at the end of October and lasts until April. In those six months, each team plays 82 games of professional basketball.

The best 16 teams then enter the playoffs from April to June. To reach the seven-game final for the NBA Championship, a team may have played as many as 103 games.

Trades and pay

Players are sometimes traded, meaning they move to different clubs. In 2007, Kevin Garnett was traded from the Minnesota Timberwolves to the Boston Celtics for seven other players, the biggest ever NBA trade for a single player.

Kobe Bryant was believed to have earned US$33 million in a single year, making him one of the world's top ten highest earning sportspeople.

Along with games, training sessions and drills to work on moves, top players are expected to meet with fans and help promote their sport all over the world.

Passing

The best way to move the ball around the court is to pass it. You can pass the ball faster than you can dribble with it. Aim your passes carefully so that they are easy for your team-mate to catch. The player catching the ball is called the receiver.

The simplest pass is the chest pass. You need to position your hands around the back and sides of the ball. Then you push the ball away from your chest. The ball leaves your hands with a flick of the wrists.

▼ To make a chest pass, bend your elbows and then straighten your arms to send the ball flying away.

▼ To make an overhead pass, raise your arms above your head. Throw the ball forward with a flick of your wrists.

▼ The flip pass is a short pass that you make with a flick of one hand.

The bounce pass is useful when there is an opponent between you and your receiver. You bounce the ball past the opponent so that it springs up and into your receiver's hands. You can make a bounce pass with one hand or two hands on the ball.

Whichever pass you use, you need to be accurate. A weak pass may get caught by an opponent. Too strong a pass might be hard for your team-mate to catch. As soon as you have passed, get moving! Move to a place on the court where you can receive a pass yourself.

Try to catch the ball using both hands. Keep your eyes on the ball as it reaches you. As soon as the ball is in your hands, bring it into your chest. This protects the ball from other players.

▼ This player uses two hands to drive the ball forward and down for a bounce pass. Aim for the ball to bounce about two thirds of the way to your receiver.

Individual skills

▲ This player is in the triple threat stance.

▲ Carlos Delfino of Argentina dribbles the ball and surges past the USA's Jason Kidd at the 2008 Olympics.

With the ball in your hands, try to get into what is called the triple threat stance. The ball is held around chest height, with the head up looking at the game and one foot ahead of the other with knees bent a little. From this position, you can do three things. You can shoot, pass to a team-mate or dribble with the ball.

Dribbling takes a lot of practice to master. You use one hand to push the ball down to the floor and collect it as it rises. Your hand must stay on the top half of the ball as you bounce it. Keep the bounce between waist and knee height if you can.

A double dribble is when you dribble the ball, catch it in your hands and then start to dribble again. You don't want to do this, as the ball will be given to the other team who will restart the game with a throw from the sideline.

▲ This player dribbles the ball. He protects the ball by putting his body between it and his opponent.

▲ This player is pivoting. He steps round to his left to get away from a defender and to find a team-mate to pass to.

When you stop dribbling or when you catch the ball, you cannot run with it in your hands. This is called travelling and it results in the ball being given to the other team. But you can keep one foot still and twist and step round using your other foot. This is called pivoting and it allows you to turn to pass in any direction on the court.

With the ball in your hand you can use a fake to trick an opponent who is close to you. You can pretend to pass to one side but instead, pass to the other. You can also pretend to pass low and then shoot or pretend to shoot but start a dribble instead.

Attacking

Attacking takes individual skills and great teamwork. Your team has to work together to get past the other team's defence and put yourselves in good positions to have a shot. If you have the ball, you have to stay alert to where your team-mates are.

When you don't have the ball, try to get into a position where your team-mates can pass to you. This often means getting away from a defender who is nearby.

▼ The player in the blue vest pretends to move one way before sprinting the other. He is then in space to receive a quick pass.

Basketball players make cuts which are short, sharp sprints. Sometimes, they drop one shoulder and lean one way but sprint in another direction to try to fool an opponent. Whenever you get free, look up at your team-mate with the ball, ready to catch a pass.

Assists

Attacking passes which lead to a team-mate scoring are called assists. John Stockton made a record 15,806 assists in his NBA career.

Magic Johnson made 10,141 assists in his NBA career, more than 11 assists per game.

Scott Skiles made the most assists ever in a single game in 1990. He made 30 for his team, the Orlando Magic.

Attacking teams try to pass the ball in close to the basket to give their team the best chance of scoring. The lay up is another way of getting really close to the basket for a shot.

This is when a player with the ball dribbles and drives towards the basket. Then the player jumps and takes a shot from close range.

▼ To make a lay up, you dribble the ball and step in close to the basket. As you leap up, you flick or push the ball up either straight towards the basket or bounce the ball off the backboard.

Defending

Defending is all about stopping the other team scoring and getting the ball back in your team's hands as soon as possible. It takes good individual skills as well as close teamwork.

There are different ways to play defence. When starting out, you are likely to mark an opposing player who doesn't have the ball. You move as he or she moves and you try to stop your opponent from getting into a space to receive the ball.

If you are marking the player with the ball, you need to get close to them. Bend your knees, face your opponent

▼ Stay alert for a weak pass from the other team. You may be able to get the ball yourself. This is called an interception.

▼ Make yourself as big as possible when marking the player with the ball. Your hands can be out to the side if you think they will pass to the side. Be ready, though, for a sudden change of movement or a shot or dribble.

▼ The defender (in white) sprints hard to stop her opponent getting away. You need a lot of energy to keep on running in defence. It is a very important part of the sport.

and stay on your toes, ready to move in any direction.

When the ball hits the hoop or the backboard it can bounce off at all sorts of angles. The skill of getting the ball in your hands at this time is called rebounding. You have to watch the ball and time your jump to get the ball before others.

Rebounding is important in basketball. For the defending players, a successful rebound means they have the ball and can start an attack. For players in an attacking team, winning a rebound means they get another chance to shoot.

▼ Yao Ming (left) and Aaron Brooks of the Houston Rockets both leap up for a rebound. To rebound well, you need to turn and face the basket and time your jump.

Team plays

A team of players works together on certain moves in attack and defence. Many of these moves are practised a lot in training so that they are slick and successful in the game.

Teams work on ways of turning defence into attack. Your team may try a fast break. This is when one player dribbles and sprints up the court. Dribblers need support from team-mates so they can pass the ball on the run.

Halfway line

▲ This complicated-looking move is actually quite simple. Called the full court press, the team in blue closes in on the team in white to try to stop the players passing or moving the ball out of their back court. If the team with the ball stays in its back court for more than 10 seconds, then the ball will be given to the other team.

▲ Jason Kidd of the USA tries to defend against Spain's Pau Gasol during the game for the 2008 Olympic gold medal. The USA won the game by 118 points to 107.

▲ Australia's Tully Bevilaqua calls and directs her team-mates. Communicating with your team is important in a game.

Another simple team attacking move is the one-two pass. You pass the ball, then sprint hard past an opponent. Your team-mate passes the ball back when you are on the other side of your opponent.

At other times, you may work as a team to make space for others. One or two of your team may move in one direction. If these players draw defenders towards them, it may create space for the player with the ball.

Basketball rules...OK!

Every sport has rules and basketball is no exception. Basketball's rules are enforced by a game's referees. They decide on everything, from which team put the ball out of play to whether a player has made a foul.

Before a game, referees check that players aren't wearing anything they shouldn't, such as jewellery. A referee starts and stops a game. A game is stopped every time the ball goes out of play or if a foul or a violation (a less serious breaking of the rules) occurs.

▲ You must not dribble and run into a player who is standing still when you have the ball. This is called a charging foul.

▲ You are not allowed to push or pull the shirt of an opponent. This is a foul.

▲
The player in blue slaps the hand of her opponent who is holding the ball. This is a foul.

Double dribbles and travelling (see pages 16-17) are examples of violations. Other violations include the ball touching your feet or your team not shooting the ball within 30 seconds (24 seconds in the NBA).

Basketball is a non-contact sport, so pushing, shoving or tripping a player are all fouls. So is using bad language to other players or officials. When a foul is signalled, the player who has made the foul raises his or her arm. Fouls usually result in the other team being given free throws.

Players fear collecting five fouls (or six in the NBA). If they do so, they are ejected. This means they are out of the game, although their team can use a substitute and play on with five players.

The world of basketball

Basketball is played all around the world at many different levels. Most of the world's basketball is run by FIBA (the International Basketball Federation). This includes basketball at the Olympics and the World Championships. Both competitions take place every four years and have contests for men's and women's teams.

▼ Michael Jordan, one of basketball's biggest stars, soars through the air towards the basket. Jordan scored an incredible 32,292 points in his NBA career.

Professional basketball is played in around 30 countries. The most famous league is the NBA. It began in the 1940s and now has 30 clubs from Canada and the USA.

The NBA is home to most of the world's greatest players. In the past, legends like Michael Jordan and Magic Johnson played in the NBA. Today's stars include LeBron James, Dwyane Wade, Kobe Bryant and Shaquille O'Neal.

Whilst most of the players in the NBA are from North America, more and more come from around the world, including China's Yao Ming, Manu Ginobili from Argentina, Spain's Pau Gasol and Dirk Nowitzki from Germany.

The WNBA professional league for women began in 1997 and features 14 teams, all based in the USA.

Big competitions

Only three of the NBA's 30 teams don't have names ending in the letter S – the Utah Jazz, the Miami Heat, and the Orlando Magic.

The first Olympic basketball final was one of the lowest scoring games ever. The outdoor court was muddy, it was raining and the final score was just 19-8. It was the United States' first of 12 men's basketball gold medals in 16 Olympics.

▼ Lisa Leslie remains the WNBA's most famous player. She was the first professional female to score a slam dunk. Slam dunks are spectacular shots made by tall players who leap above the basket and stuff the ball through the hoop.

Where next?

These websites and books will help you to find out more about basketball.

Websites

http://www.ncaa.org/bbp/basketball_marketing/kids_club/
This section of the NCAA basketball website contains video clips of basic skills, coaching tips and fun basketball games to play.

http://www.hoophall.com/
This website tells you all about the over 250 players and coaches who are found in the Naismith Basketball Hall of Fame.

http://www.harlemglobetrotters.com/photos/videos/
Watch videos of their tricks and learn all about the most famous show team in basketball history – the Harlem Globetrotters.

http://www.mini-basketball.org.uk/
This website has the rules and tips on skills needed to play mini basketball.

http://www.sikids.com/
Keep up to date with all the teams and scores from the NBA and NCAA at Sports Illustrated's fun website especially for children.

www.fiba.com
This is the official website of the International Basketball Federation.

http://aol.wnba.com/
The official website of the women's professional basketball competition. The website contains lots of facts, profiles of the best players and videos of the action.

Books

Know Your Sport: Basketball – Clive Gifford (Franklin Watts, 2008)

How to Improve at Basketball – Jim Drewett (Crabtree Publishing, 2007).

Basketball words

assist a pass which leads directly to a team-mate scoring a basket

backboard the rectangular piece of wood or other material to which the hoop and net are fixed

bounce pass a pass in which the basketball bounces about two-thirds of the way from the passer to the receiver

double dribble a move in which a player dribbles the ball, catches it and then starts to dribble again. A double dribble is a violation

dribbling bouncing the basketball continuously

free throw a shot from in front of the basket awarded by the referee for a foul by the other team

jump ball a way of starting or restarting the game. A referee throws the ball into the air and one player from each side jumps for it

lay up a close up shot

rebounding jumping up and winning the ball after a failed attempt at a shot

three pointer a successful shot which is worth three points because the shot is taken from beyond the three point line

tip-off the start of the game with a jump ball

travelling taking too many steps after catching the ball. Travelling is a violation

violation a breaking of one of the rules of basketball. A violation is not as serious as a foul

Index

Numbers in **bold** refer to pictures.